Who Is Bruce Springsteen?

by Stephanie Sabol

illustrated by Gregory Copeland

Penguin Workshop

For Mom and Dad—SS

To my dear friends Souch and Jen—GC

PENGUIN WORKSHOP
An Imprint of Penguin Random House LLC, New York

If you purchased this book without a cover, you should be aware that this book is stolen property. It was reported as "unsold and destroyed" to the publisher, and neither the author nor the publisher has received any payment for this "stripped book."

Penguin supports copyright. Copyright fuels creativity, encourages diverse voices, promotes free speech, and creates a vibrant culture. Thank you for buying an authorized edition of this book and for complying with copyright laws by not reproducing, scanning, or distributing any part of it in any form without permission. You are supporting writers and allowing Penguin to continue to publish books for every reader.

The publisher does not have any control over and does not assume any responsibility for author or third-party websites or their content.

Text copyright © 2016 by Stephanie Sabol.
Illustrations copyright © 2016 by Penguin Random House LLC. All rights reserved.
Published by Penguin Workshop, an imprint of Penguin Random House LLC, New York.
PENGUIN and PENGUIN WORKSHOP are trademarks of Penguin Books Ltd.
WHO HQ & Design is a registered trademark of Penguin Random House LLC.
Printed in the USA.

Visit us online at www.penguinrandomhouse.com.

Library of Congress Control Number: 2016033272

ISBN 9780448487038 10 9 8 7 6

Contents

MUSIC SHO
$60
MERRY
CHRISTMAS

Who Is Bruce Springsteen?

December 1964

It was a cold winter day in northern New Jersey. A teenage boy brought his mother to the local music store. There, in the front window, was a black and gold electric guitar. The boy wanted it so much. He loved to play the guitar. But it cost sixty dollars. Back then, that was a lot of money. It was more money than his mother had. So they left the store without the guitar.

But that is not the end of the story.

A few days later, the boy's mother went to the bank and took out a loan. On Christmas Day, her son woke up to find the guitar waiting for him under the tree.

That teenage boy was Bruce Springsteen. And he grew up to become one of the most famous rock-and-roll stars ever. For forty years, people have been inspired by the messages in his songs. They are songs about the joy of being alive and the pain of a broken heart. They offer comfort during hard times. They make people proud to be Americans.

Bruce Springsteen never forgot that special guitar. It changed everything. In fact, when he was voted into the Rock and Roll Hall of Fame in 1999, the first person he thanked was his mother. He thanked her for buying him that guitar and, most importantly, for believing in him.

CHAPTER 1
A Young Boy

Bruce Frederick Springsteen was born on September 23, 1949. He lived in Freehold, New Jersey, with his parents and two younger sisters, Virginia (called Ginny) and Pamela. Ginny was one and a half years younger than Bruce, but Pamela was much younger. Bruce was twelve when Pamela was born. Pamela was such a cute baby that Bruce didn't mind helping out.

He liked playing with her or even giving her a bottle.

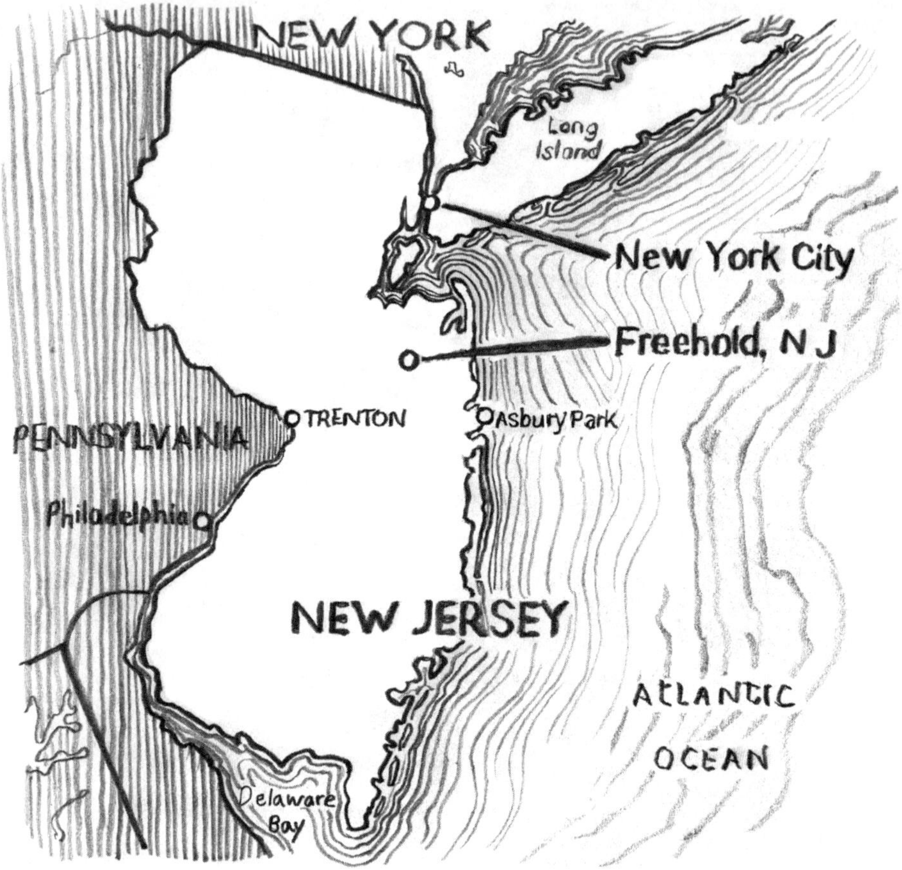

Freehold is a medium-size town located near the New Jersey shoreline, and about a ninety-minute drive from New York City. There were lots of farms and factories when Bruce was a boy. It was not a wealthy town. People in Freehold were mostly "blue collar" workers.

Blue Collar Workers

The name "blue collar" comes from the color of denim work shirts worn by men who have low-paying jobs—jobs in a garage or on a factory assembly line, for example. "White collar" describes workers who make more money. They work in offices where they need to dress up in shirts with white collars.

Most of the jobs in Freehold were at the local factories. The biggest was Nestlé, which produced chocolate bars and coffee. While Bruce was growing up, one of the big employers, a rug factory, left town. Jobs became harder to find. Bruce's mother, Adele, worked as a secretary for a lawyer. She had a good job. However, Bruce's father, Doug, had trouble finding steady work. For a while he drove taxis and trucks. At one point he was a prison guard.

To make ends meet, the Springsteens moved in with Doug's parents after Bruce was born. They stayed for six years. Bruce's grandparents lived in a house that had cracked walls, windows that rattled, and just one kerosene heater to warm the house in winter. His grandparents didn't believe in a lot of rules for him. Bruce was allowed to stay up all night, watching television and playing with his toys.

As a little boy, Bruce loved to have books read aloud to him. One of his favorites was *Brave Cowboy Bill*. Bill had many adventures in the Wild West. Bruce was so crazy about the story that soon he knew all the words by heart.

When Bruce was old enough, his mother sent him to a Catholic school. Bruce did not like it one bit! There were so many rules, and the nuns were very strict. One time in third grade, a nun stuffed him in a trash can!

Why?

She said the trash can was where he belonged. As if he were no better than garbage! Bruce spent time in the principal's office, too.

He was not a bad kid. He was just different. He liked to be alone with his thoughts. Not all the time, of course. He also liked to hang out with other kids, play baseball, and read Archie comics.

Bruce enjoyed spending time with his mother. Adele also loved music. She'd play the radio in the kitchen, singing and dancing while making breakfast. Bruce sang and danced right along with her.

Adele introduced Bruce to all kinds of music—pop, rock and roll, country, and folk music. One night in 1957, Adele let Bruce stay up late to watch *The Ed Sullivan Show* on television. Elvis Presley was performing, and Bruce could not take his eyes off him. Elvis wasn't afraid to be different,

and he looked like he was having so much fun onstage. After seeing Elvis, Bruce wanted his own guitar. If Elvis could be a rock star, why couldn't he?

As Bruce grew older, all he could think about was rock-and-roll music. When he was fourteen, he was riding in the car with his mom, listening to the radio. The Beatles song "I Want to Hold Your Hand" started to play.

Elvis Presley

Elvis Aaron Presley was born in Tupelo, Mississippi, in 1935 and died in 1977. He learned to sing and play the guitar at his church. He would grow up to become known as the "King of Rock and Roll."

Before rock and roll, there was music called rhythm and blues, or R&B. It was popular with black musicians. Elvis loved the smooth sound of R&B. It was fun to dance to and had a steady beat. Elvis shook his hips when he danced. When he went onstage, the fans screamed with happiness.

Elvis had a very fancy mansion in Memphis, Tennessee, called Graceland. It had eight bathrooms and a garage full of antique cars. In 1976, Bruce tried to sneak into Graceland! He wanted to meet Elvis, his idol. The guards sent him away. Elvis wasn't home.

As soon as Bruce's mom stopped the car, Bruce jumped out and ran to the nearest pay phone. He had to call his girlfriend. He couldn't wait to tell her about the awesome song he had just heard.

Then, in 1964, Bruce got that special guitar for Christmas. From then on, Bruce practiced every day. He said, "It took over my whole life. . . . Everything from then on revolved around music. Everything." Sometimes Bruce would play the guitar and watch himself in the mirror. Even though Bruce was just a skinny boy with dark curly hair, he liked what he saw. When he held his guitar, he felt powerful.

CHAPTER 2
Practice Makes Perfect

After Bruce finished the eighth grade in 1963, he switched to a big public high school in Freehold. Bruce still mostly kept to himself. He didn't care much about the other kids or his classes. Sometimes he would sneak out of class to practice guitar in the band room. He taught himself to play "Twist and Shout" the way the Beatles played it.

Bruce would practice for hours—sometimes for ten hours a day! He wasn't interested in drinking or doing drugs, because he felt it would take him away from his music. Bruce started to grow his hair long because some of his favorite rock stars did. He wanted to look like a rocker, too.

Some boys in Bruce's high school had a band. One day, Bruce heard the band was looking for a new guitar player. There was a tryout.

Bruce showed up and played some music. He mostly played bits and pieces of some popular songs from the radio. The band was not impressed. The boys sent him home. But Bruce didn't let that stop him. That night he taught himself a whole set of complete songs. He went back to the band the next day. He played six new songs perfectly. Bruce was in the band!

The band was named the Castiles. Castile was a kind of soap that was popular with teenage boys. The band played at school dances, swim clubs, and at "Battle of the Bands" contests.

They even went to Manhattan to play at Cafe Wha? It was a famous club in Greenwich Village where Bob Dylan and Jimi Hendrix had played.

This meant a lot to Bruce because Bob Dylan was one of his idols. Bruce admired the words of Dylan's songs. They were like long poems or stories.

Bob Dylan

And Dylan was great at so many kinds of music—rock, folk, and blues.

Bruce played with the Castiles throughout high school. On the morning of graduation, Bruce went to pick up his cap and gown. But there was a problem. A teacher said that Bruce had to cut his shoulder-length hair or he would not get into the ceremony. That made Bruce mad. He decided to skip graduation. Instead, he took a two-hour bus ride to Manhattan and listened to bands at different music clubs. Bruce's mom was disappointed. She had planned a big party for him! But Bruce wanted to do his own thing.

It was 1967. After high school, many of Bruce's classmates went on to college. Others took full-time jobs or joined the army. Bruce wasn't sure what he wanted to do—other than play music with the Castiles. So he ended up going to a local college where he once again felt like an outsider. Hardly anybody

else had such long hair or wore glasses with yellow lenses. Still there was one place where Bruce felt at ease: his writing class. He received As on some of his short stories, and his teacher encouraged him to write more. Bruce discovered the power of words.

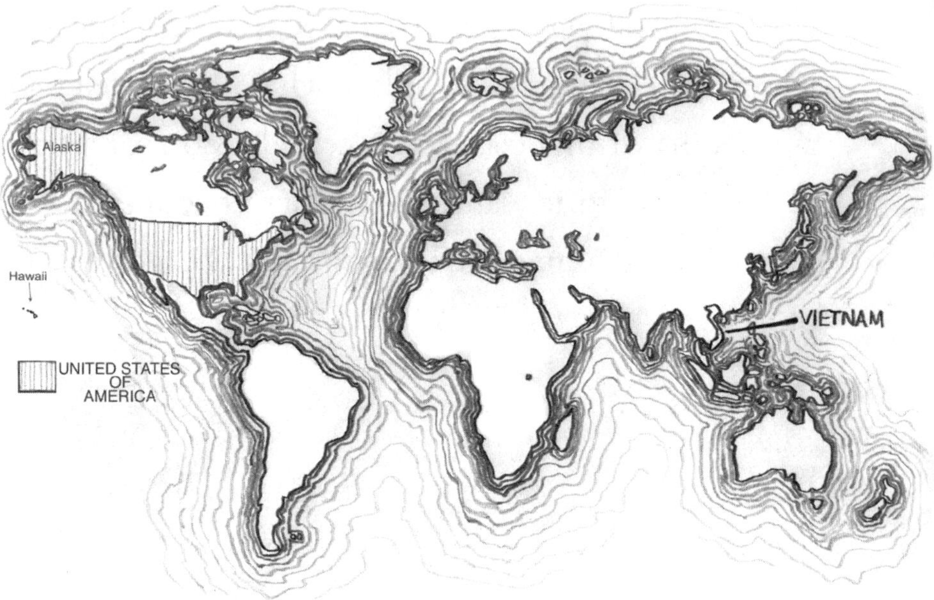

Still, college wasn't for Bruce. He dropped out in his second year. It was 1969. The United States was in the middle of a war far away in Vietnam, a small country in Southeast Asia. Young men Bruce's age were being sent to fight. It didn't matter if they wanted to be in the army or not. It didn't matter if they believed in the war or not. If you were drafted—that meant picked—to join the army, you went.

Like all young men, Bruce had to be examined by a doctor before serving in the army. Bruce was against the war and did not want to fight. So he figured out a way to make the army reject him.

The army didn't want anybody crazy to become a soldier, so Bruce decided to act crazy. During his exam, he said strange things that made no sense. It worked. Bruce failed the exam and never became a soldier. Later, Bruce was ashamed about failing his exam on purpose. Years later he told a concert audience that "It ain't nothin' to applaud about."

It was at this point that Bruce decided to make music his full-time career. He wasn't going to take any other job, not if he could help it. The Castiles had broken up, so Bruce began to play solo gigs in a small beach town called Asbury Park. It was there that people really began to notice Bruce. Not only did he sing and play the guitar, he also knew harmonica and the piano.

Bruce's sound was unique. It was rock and roll but had bits of jazz, soul, and Latin music in it, too. When Bruce performed, everyone in the room stopped to listen.

Asbury Park

The seaside community of Asbury Park is located on the coast of New Jersey. In the late 1800s, the town was developed as a vacation resort. Each summer, people would take the train from New York City or Philadelphia to enjoy the town's beaches, boardwalk, amusement park rides, and shopping. Asbury Park's annual baby parade had fifty thousand spectators!

After World War II, Asbury Park had fewer visitors. Buildings fell down and crime increased. However, the music scene in Asbury Park began to grow. Musicians would come to play rock and roll, rhythm and blues, and doo-wop at the local clubs and bars. The Stone Pony, one of the most famous music venues, opened in 1974.

Today, Asbury Park is once more like the vacation spot it was over a hundred years ago. Music remains a big part of the scene, and the Stone Pony is still open. Sometimes Bruce even stops by to play!

CHAPTER 3
Jersey Shore Fame

One of the clubs in Asbury Park was called Upstage. Above a shoe store, it was a place where music groups played all night long. The walls were painted in neon colors, and black lights hung down from the ceiling. One evening Bruce walked in and politely asked the owner if he could play. He was told to go onstage and set up his equipment. So that's what Bruce did.

Bruce started playing and suddenly the room became very quiet. The audience stopped chatting and listened to the scrawny kid with long dark curls. They whispered about how good he was.

He had a low gravelly voice that came from deep in his throat. He was serious, but had energy and charm. The audience knew they were watching someone special.

Some people in the audience were musicians themselves. When Bruce finished, a few of them jumped onstage with him to play. It turned out they wanted to start a band with Bruce. Was Bruce cool with that? Absolutely!

Bruce and three other guys named the new band Child. They liked that name because it meant the beginning of something new.

The band hired a manager who also owned a surfboard factory. Bruce lived in the factory, and the band rehearsed there, too. Sometimes they even helped make surfboards!

Child played in Asbury Park and at clubs in other towns nearby. Soon they had a loyal following of college students. But it turned out there was another band named Child. They played in New York and had already made an album. So Bruce's band had no choice but to change its name. They became known as Steel Mill.

Steel Mill grew more and more popular. They began to get jobs outside of New Jersey. They had lots of fans in Richmond, Virginia,

Bruce's Bands through the Years

Bruce was part of many groups before the E Street Band. Among them:

1. The Castiles: Bruce joined this band when he was fifteen years old. He played with the Castiles from 1965 until 1968, when they broke up.

2. Earth: Earth played together for six months between summer 1968 and winter 1969.

3. Child/Steel Mill: Child was formed in 1969, changed its named to Steel Mill, and played together until 1971.

4. Dr. Zoom and the Sonic Zoom: This large band had more than ten members but didn't last long—they only played two shows!

5. **Bruce Springsteen Band: As the name says, Bruce was the main guy in the group.**

6. **E Street Band: The most famous of Bruce's bands, the E Street Band included many members of Bruce's earlier bands. Bruce has played with this band for over forty years.**

which was five hours away by car. They also booked some shows in San Francisco, California. San Francisco was where famous bands like the Grateful Dead had started out.

Although Steel Mill had a

The Grateful Dead

loyal following, one thing was clear: Bruce was the star. He was the reason that people came to hear Steel Mill. Bruce's bandmates knew it, too. But Bruce liked to be fair. After every show, Bruce divided up the money. Everyone in the band received the same amount. Even though he wasn't paid more, the others began calling him "The Boss." Bruce never liked that nickname! Nevertheless, it stuck.

In the fall of 1971, Bruce turned twenty-two. Over the past six years he had always been in a group. But now Bruce wanted to break away and become a star on his own. He got in touch with a record producer in New York City named Mike Appel. Mike listened to Bruce sing and play two songs.

Mike Appel

Mike thought Bruce had potential, but he told him to learn more songs and work on his songwriting. He sent Bruce away.

Bruce left the meeting disappointed but not defeated. He wrote more songs, and three months later, he returned to play for Appel again. This time the reaction was different. Appel was speechless after hearing some of Bruce's new songs. Bruce's performance seemed magical. One fast-paced song was called "It's Hard to Be a Saint in the City." It was about a tough guy living on the streets of a city. The lyrics were intense, and the melodies were unique. After hearing this song, Appel wanted to be Bruce's manager. He was convinced Bruce was going to be the next big rock-and-roll star!

A few months later, Mike arranged a meeting between Bruce and a very important executive at Columbia Records named John Hammond.

John Hammond

Hammond had discovered Bob Dylan. He made jazz singer Billie Holiday a star, as well as folksinger Pete Seeger. Hammond listened to Bruce play for two hours. He was excited but he kept his cool. When Bruce was done, Hammond nodded and then asked if Bruce could play that night at a club in downtown Manhattan. Hammond wanted to see how Bruce performed in front of an audience. Bruce didn't think twice before saying yes.

That night, Bruce sang and played a few songs for a small crowd at the Gaslight at the Au Go Go.

If Bruce was nervous, he didn't show it. He told some jokes to the audience while he tuned his guitar. Bruce only played a few songs, but he was charming and full of energy.

Later that night, Hammond told Bruce that his life was about to change. Columbia Records was signing him up! Bruce called his parents and told them the great news. Bruce's mom was overjoyed. Bruce wasn't too close to his father, but even he was excited. This was the beginning of the big time.

CHAPTER 4
Becoming a Star

Now Bruce had a record label behind him. Why was that a big deal? First of all, a record label helped musicians create albums. They had studios where musicians recorded songs. Audio engineers helped make the music sound as good as it could be.

Designers created the album covers. A publicity department helped get songs played on the radio stations. And salespeople got the music stores to keep the album in stock. Back in the 1970s, there were lots of music stores. People weren't able to buy music online or on their iPods. But then as now, the record label and the musician worked together to make the best album and sell as many copies as possible.

Bruce asked a few of his bandmates from Steel Mill to record the album with him. In time, this new band would be known as the E Street Band. The band got their name because they sometimes practiced on E Street in a New Jersey beach town called Belmar.

Members of the E Street Band came and went. Some played with the band for years. Others joined only for special tours. Over the years there were more than a dozen members of the E Street Band. The most well-known players were Clarence Clemons on the saxophone, Steve Van Zandt on the guitar, and Max Weinberg on the drums.

Most-Famous E Street Band Members

Clarence Clemons

Clarence Clemons was born in 1942 in Virginia. He received his first saxophone when he was nine years old. Bruce and Clarence met one rainy night in Asbury Park and immediately liked each other. Clarence was known for his solo saxophone performances—some that lasted several minutes. He was also known as the "Big Man" because he was well over six feet tall!

Steve Van Zandt

Steve Van Zandt was born in 1950 in Massachusetts, but moved to New Jersey as a boy. He mostly played the guitar for the E Street Band but also sang backup with Bruce and played the mandolin. Many people know Steve from his role as an actor. He played a mobster in a popular television series, *The Sopranos*, from 1999 to 2007. Steve had never acted before he joined the show!

Max Weinberg was born in 1951 in Newark, New Jersey. He started to play the drums when he was six years old. Max planned on becoming a lawyer but he dropped out of college when he was offered a job with the E Street Band. In the early 1990s, Max became the leader of the "house band" for late-night television host Conan O'Brien. He and his band played for the show almost every weeknight for nearly seventeen years.

Max Weinberg

Bruce's first album came out in 1973. It was called *Greetings from Asbury Park, N.J.* Bruce spent hours recording with the band to make each of the nine songs perfect. "Growin' Up" was a fast-paced tune about a teenage boy breaking all the rules. Bruce sang the lyrics "When they said 'sit down,' I stood up!" It was easy to see he was singing about his own teenage years.

Many people at Columbia Records were very excited for the album release. Some of the publicists and salespeople had become fans of Bruce themselves. They loved the way Bruce told stories in his music. Bruce sang about regular people who had good times and bad times. His lyrics made people feel hopeful and alive. When "Blinded by the Light" or "Spirit in the Night"

played, it was easy to feel the energy of the lyrics.

Unfortunately, the album did not sell well. Another album came out the same day. It was by a group called the Partridge Family. The Partridge Family wasn't a real family—they were actors in a popular television show about a family band with the same name. Their music was peppy and sounded like music for a commercial.

The Partridge Family album sold more copies than Bruce's did—even in Bruce's hometown music store. Ten months later, Bruce released a second album. This one didn't sell much better.

This was not good news. The executives at Columbia were getting nervous. Bruce needed an album with a hit song. And so far there hadn't been one. They decided to give him one more chance. Columbia would give Bruce enough money to record just one more song, not a whole album. The song had to feel like a hit to the record producers, one that the radio stations would play over and over. People might hear the song on the radio and decide to buy the album.

The pressure was on. Bruce knew this could be his last chance at success. He started to work on a new song. It told the story of a girl and boy wanting to escape their boring lives for something more exciting. The music had a pounding beat that got stuck in your head and wouldn't leave. Bruce worked on the song for a few months. He called it "Born to Run," and it ran nearly five minutes long. Bruce's throaty voice along with the guitars, keyboard, saxophone, and drums came together to create an explosive sound that made people want to jump up and dance! The chorus line, "Tramps like us, baby, we were born to run!" would become one of Bruce's famous lyrics.

"Born to Run" was going to be a hit. Everyone at Columbia was sure of it. Bruce was told to go write more songs and complete a third album. At around the same time, a music critic named Jon Landau saw Bruce perform at the Harvard Square Theater in Cambridge, Massachusetts. The next day he wrote a review in a Boston newspaper. He said, "I saw rock and roll's future and its name is Bruce Springsteen."

Jon Landau with Bruce

After this, Columbia planned a big concert tour for Bruce's new album. Ads appeared in newspapers, and big displays were created for music stores. Excitement was building.

The name of the album was *Born to Run*—the same as the title of the song Bruce worked so long on. When *Born to Run* went on sale in 1975, it started selling a lot of copies right away. *Born to Run* reached number three on the *Billboard* charts. *Billboard* is a magazine that keeps track of music sales.

Weekly newsmagazines were interested in writing about Bruce, too. The two biggest, *Time* and *Newsweek*, both put Bruce on their covers and ran stories on him. This was very unusual.

Magazines don't like to have the same stories. But Bruce Springsteen's music demanded attention!

Bruce shot up to stardom once *Born to Run* came out. With his new success, Bruce was ready to work even harder. He said, "More than rich, more than famous, more than happy, I wanted to be great."

CHAPTER 5
The Sounds of Success

Bruce and the band went on several concert tours for *Born to Run*. In total, they played more than two hundred shows in the United States, Canada, and Europe.

In the early days of the band, before their first album was released, they didn't have much money for tours. One time they played some shows in Boston and stayed at a friend's house—they had to take turns sleeping on a few mattresses in the attic!

As the band became famous, they were able to travel more comfortably. Sometimes Bruce and the band stayed in expensive hotels and ate fancy food. But most of the time they stayed at average places. It was important to Bruce to remain a regular guy. His fans loved him for that. He wasn't a big party animal, either. On one tour, the band had two buses that took them to shows—a party bus and quiet bus. Bruce preferred to stay in the quiet bus where he could sleep.

Often rock stars will perform for about an hour and a half at concerts. Not Bruce. He'd be on the stage for over three hours—singing, dancing, and telling stories in between songs. Sometimes he would talk about his family or the house where he grew up. Sometimes he talked about the girls he had crushes on. The audience went wild. They felt connected to Bruce. He seemed to be telling them that he was like them. His memories almost felt like their memories. Bruce knew how important it was to connect with his audience. He has said, "An audience is not brought to you or given to you; it's something that you fight for."

After the success of *Born to Run*, Bruce finally had money. He rented a big farmhouse in New

Jersey where the band could rehearse. He also bought himself a 1957 Chevy. It was yellow with bright orange flames running down the sides. Bruce loved it, but soon his fans began to recognize the car. When they saw him driving by, they chased after the car!

Even with his busy schedule, Bruce still liked to spend time by himself. After the *Born to Run* tour finished, he put aside more time for his writing. Bruce wasn't a big reader. Instead, he preferred watching movies. He studied how they told stories and tried to do the same in his songwriting.

John Steinbeck

One of the films that inspired him was *The Grapes of Wrath.* It was based on the book by John Steinbeck. *The Grapes of Wrath* showed the struggle of poor people in America during the 1930s. The struggle of working-class people was very important to Bruce. He wanted his songs to show how hard and lonely life could be in places like Freehold, where he had grown up.

Bruce also looked to other singers for inspiration. He very much admired the folksinger Woody Guthrie. Woody's songs were about life in the 1930s. During the worst years of the Great Depression, one out of every four working people was unemployed in the United States.

Woody Guthrie

Woody Guthrie was one of America's most famous folksingers. Born in 1912 in Oklahoma, Woody had a difficult childhood. His family lost all their money, his sister died suddenly, and his mother was very sick. Woody and his siblings were left to fend for themselves. When the Great Depression hit, Woody traveled west to find a job. On the road, Woody played his harmonica and guitar for people who were also looking for jobs. He sang about how hard it was to be poor.

Woody wrote many songs about everyday life in America. Songs like "This Land Is Your Land" had strong messages. Although Woody died in 1967, his music has inspired many songwriters, like Bob Dylan and Bruce Springsteen.

Woody Guthrie's most famous song was "This Land Is Your Land." The lyrics call for an America where everyone is equal no matter how rich or poor they are. Guthrie was considered a voice of his time.

Between 1976 and 1983, Bruce and the E Street Band released three more albums. They played over 250 shows on tour. The albums sold well, but none was as popular as *Born to Run* had been. Then in 1984, the band exploded with another album. This one was called *Born in the U.S.A.*

When the record executives heard *Born in the U.S.A.,* they were thrilled. The album was full of songs that had "hit" written all over them. "Dancing in the Dark" and "Glory Days" were just the kinds of catchy songs that people would listen to again and again. Radio stations were going to jump on these songs. Even more people would become die-hard fans of Bruce Springsteen.

"Born in the U.S.A." was the name of both the album and one of the hit songs. The song had a pounding rhythm that repeated itself when Bruce sang the words "Born in the U.S.A.!" When people heard the song, they felt proud to be American. The funny thing was, Bruce didn't even mean for the song to be understood that way—it was supposed to be about the sad and terrible effects of the Vietnam War.

Born in the U.S.A. was huge. It was the best-selling album of 1985. Seven out of the ten songs were hit singles. *Born in the U.S.A.* would become Diamond Platinum. That meant it sold more than ten million copies. More important than sales, though, *Born in the U.S.A.* made Bruce an even bigger star. People all over the world knew Bruce now, not just people in New Jersey or the United States. He was the rock star who wore blue jeans, a white T-shirt, and a bandanna around his head. He was a working-class hero, although one who was also a millionaire!

CHAPTER 6
Family Man

Bruce lived and breathed for his music. It didn't leave much time for romance or love. Throughout his life, Bruce had had girlfriends. He had never gotten married, though. That changed in 1985. Bruce was thirty-five when he met an actress named Julianne Phillips. Juli was ten years younger than Bruce. She had grown up in Oregon, the youngest of six children. She had been a model before she was an actress.

Julianne Phillips

Bruce and Juli got married just seven months after they met. Bruce told one of his friends that the first time he saw Juli, he knew she was the one for him.

Unfortunately, he was wrong. The marriage was a difficult one. Bruce and Juli spent a lot of time apart. Bruce was on tour with the band, and Juli focused on her acting.

A few years after they were married, Bruce and Juli separated, and Bruce began seeing Patti Scialfa.

Patti Scialfa

A Jersey Shore native, Patti was a backup singer for the E Street Band. When Bruce and Patti started dating, some fans were upset because Bruce and Juli weren't divorced yet. But it turned out that Patti Scialfa *was* the right person for Bruce. They married a few years later.

Besides ending his first marriage, Bruce wanted to make other changes in his life. In 1989, Bruce called the band members together. He had decided it was time for him to break away. He wanted to be on his own, not be tied to the music of the E Street Band. Some of the band members had guessed this might happen. Bruce had been pulling away from them. They knew he wanted the freedom to play solo or with different musicians. Still, they were upset that something so great was ending.

Bruce was always known as a Jersey guy. Very few performers are so closely linked with a particular state. It was the only state he had ever called home. Yet now Bruce wanted to break away from his roots. Bruce decided to move away. He and Patti moved across the country to Los Angeles.

Bruce's parents had also moved to California in the late 1960s. It was during this time that Bruce became closer with his father. His dad had suffered a stroke and was now reaching out to his son in a way he never had before.

In 1990, Bruce and Patti became parents to a son named Evan. In 1991, their daughter, Jessica, was born, and then in 1994, a son named Sam arrived. Bruce enjoyed being a father. Even though he was famous, Bruce liked doing ordinary family things, like taking his kids to school or the park. He also worked out at the local gym instead of a fancy one with superstar members. As much as possible, he wanted a normal life.

Although Bruce was no longer on tour night after night, he still worked hard on his music. During the 1990s, Bruce released three solo albums. They sold well, but not at the same pace as some of his mega-hit albums with the E Street Band. That was okay with Bruce. He liked testing out new ideas with his music.

For instance, Bruce worked on a song for a movie. Bruce's song "Streets of Philadelphia" was sad and touching. The movie, called *Philadelphia*, was about a gay man struggling with the disease AIDS. The song reached number nine on the *Billboard* charts. It sold more than half a million copies in the United States alone. Even more special, though, Bruce won an Academy Award for "Best Song" from a movie.

Eventually, Bruce was ready to return to New Jersey. He, Patti, and the kids moved to a big house not too far from Freehold. Maybe returning to his old stomping grounds made Bruce miss playing with the E Street Band, because suddenly he had an idea. What if the band came together for a reunion tour? There was no new album, but they still could play their old hits together. He wasn't sure it would work, but he and the band decided to give it a try. The results were fantastic.

The band played over 130 shows in fifteen months, from April 1999 through July 2000. The E Street Band was back together!

CHAPTER 7
Making a Difference

Bruce Springsteen was now a rock-and-roll superstar. He had a great family and had earned more money than he ever dreamed possible. Bruce wanted to make a difference. He believed rock music could change the world. He said, "I had serious ideas about rock music. Yeah, it was a circus and fun and a dance party—all of those things—but still a serious thing. I believed that serious things could be done with it. It had a power; it had a voice."

September 11, 2001, was a terrible day for the United States. Almost three thousand innocent people lost their lives in terrorist attacks in New York City, Pennsylvania, and Washington, DC.

Bruce was hit hard by the events, just like the

rest of the country. A few days later, Bruce was walking along the beach when he heard a man yell out to him. "Bruce!" the man said. "We need you!" Bruce understood what the man meant. Bruce's music had a way of helping people feel better during hard times.

Many of those who had lost their lives on September 11 were from New Jersey. Some of them had been listening to Bruce Springsteen's music for decades. When Bruce heard about these fans, he'd place a surprise phone call to one of their loved ones to pay his respects. This small gesture gave comfort to those who were suffering.

Even before the attacks, Bruce had started working on a new album. Now, though, he felt compelled to create an album to comfort people as well as inspire them. He wanted to write songs that would unite Americans. He wanted to give them a feeling of hope and a sense of belonging.

September 11

On September 11, 2001, nineteen men hijacked, or seized control of, four US passenger airplanes. Two planes hit and destroyed the Twin Towers in New York City; one struck the Pentagon outside of Washington, DC; and the fourth plane crashed in a field in western Pennsylvania. Nearly three thousand people were killed. The men who hijacked the planes were terrorists belonging to a group called al-Qaeda. Terrorists use violence to frighten people into doing what they say.

The September 11 attacks showed the worst in people. It was an awful day for the world. But good deeds happened that day, too. Strangers took care of one another. Firefighters, police officers, and citizens worked together to save lives.

The album was called *The Rising* and was recorded with the E Street Band. This was the first time the E Street Band had produced a new album together in over eighteen years! It came out in July 2002,

almost one year after the attacks. *The Rising* was a smashing success. It sold over a half million copies its first week. It was Bruce's best-selling album since *Born in the U.S.A.* Bruce and the band went on another long tour—this time they played 120 shows in over eighty cities in fourteen months.

Why was the *Rising* tour such a hit? Fans at the concerts felt a range of emotions. The lyrics of the title song, "The Rising," made them feel hopeful, while quieter songs like "You're Missing" made them stop and think about losing someone they loved. Bruce and the band knew how important their music was. E Street Band drummer Max Weinberg said, "Playing for a country that was so much in pain from the events of 9/11 made the *Rising* tour so much more than a series of rock concerts. People looked to us—actually they looked to the music—to quiet their sorrows. . . . How could rock musicians meet these expectations? But somehow we did it."

Bruce's music and lyrics made people feel good. But they were not the only way Bruce tried to help people. He also supported many causes over the years.

Bruce devoted himself to helping the poor and their struggle with hunger. Often at concerts, he asked fans to donate cans of food. Volunteers would wait by the doors and collect the food. Then they would bring it to the local food bank in the city where Bruce was playing. Thousands of cans were collected at each show.

Another cause close to Bruce's heart was supporting the American men and women who served in the armed forces. He made a special effort to help out veterans who had fought in Vietnam. (Veterans are people who have served in the military.) Bruce wasn't proud of the way he had avoided the army as a teenager. He saw many Vietnam War veterans return to the United States injured and without a job or a home. Often they did not even receive good medical care.

In 1981, Bruce met the man in charge of the Vietnam Veterans of America (VVA). The VVA raised money to support war veterans. At that time, the VVA was struggling. So Bruce performed a benefit concert in August.

All the money from the concert went to the VVA. He invited war veterans to sit next to the stage and gave a powerful speech about helping them. The event raised a lot of money. The VVA stayed open.

Bruce also wanted a change in laws dealing with immigrants—people who moved to the United States from another country. Many chose to move to find a better life with more opportunities. Bruce felt that people of all races should have a chance to live the American dream. But he worried that the rules about remaining in the United States made it too hard for certain people. Some of his songs reflect his feelings about immigration. "Matamoros Banks" tells the sad story of an immigrant who drowned crossing the river between Mexico and Texas.

Bruce had different ways of showing support for his causes. Sometimes he would quietly donate a lot of money. Sometimes he wrote songs about what he believed in and let his lyrics speak for themselves. He believed in the power of music to change people's opinions and bring out their better nature. And sometimes he would take a few minutes at his concerts to urge the crowds to support the causes he believed in.

Bruce used his voice for more than just singing.

Bruce performing at an Amnesty International concert with Tracy Chapman and Sting

CHAPTER 8
Politics

When Bruce was a boy, his family didn't talk about politics a lot. His mother told him that since they were "working people," they were Democrats. She said that because the Democratic Party has a long history of passing laws to help the poor. But Bruce never really thought much about politics or the purpose of government.

For most of his career, Bruce kept his feelings about political issues out of his music. But in 2003, the United States invaded the country of Iraq in the Middle East. As with Vietnam, Bruce didn't think the United States needed to be in this war. Bruce knew that a lot of his fans respected his opinion. It was time for him to speak his mind.

In the 2004 presidential election, Bruce threw his support behind John Kerry, the Democratic candidate. John Kerry had fought in the Vietnam War. He had met Bruce twenty-three years earlier at a Vietnam veterans benefit. Now Bruce and the E Street band led a concert tour called the Vote for Change tour. During the tour, other groups like Pearl Jam and the Dixie Chicks played concerts, too. The goal was to inspire people to go out and vote for John Kerry.

John Kerry

John Kerry lost to George W. Bush in the 2004 presidential election. But Kerry's defeat did not end Bruce's commitment to politics.

KERRY
to the

A few years later he read a book called *Dreams from My Father*. It was written by Barack Obama, who was then a US senator from Illinois. The book described Obama's life and his search to discover his roots. Bruce was inspired by Obama's words.

When Obama ran for president in 2008, Bruce gave the young senator his support. Bruce posted an endorsement of Obama on his website. He wrote, "He speaks to the America I've envisioned in my music for the past 35 years." Obama was pleased to have Bruce behind him. He even joked with his wife, Michelle, that the reason he was running for president was because he couldn't be Bruce Springsteen!

Bruce spoke at a campaign rally for Barack Obama just two days before the 2008 election.

He told the crowds that he always saw America as a place where everyone had the right to a job, an education, and a home. He said, "I want my country back. I want my dream back. I want my America back! Now is the time to stand up with Barack Obama . . . roll up our sleeves, and come on up for the rising."

Barack Obama won the election two days later, becoming the first African American elected president of the United States.

CHAPTER 9
Not Slowing Down

Bruce was getting older, but that didn't mean he was slowing down! Between 2004 and 2014, Bruce released six new albums. In his sixties, he was still a highly energetic performer. He'd still play three-hour shows, running along the stage and then sliding on his knees. Bruce brought fans onstage to sing with him. Sometimes Bruce even crowd-surfed!

In 2009, Bruce and his band performed in the halftime show at the Super Bowl.

The band played their hits for twelve minutes in Tampa, Florida, when the Pittsburgh Steelers played the Arizona Cardinals. There were over seventy thousand people at the stadium and over one hundred million people saw the show on television. Bruce and the E Street Band had come a long way from their small shows in Asbury Park.

The band celebrated the good times, but there were sad times, too. In 2008, Danny Federici passed away from cancer. Danny played the organ and accordion in the E Street Band.

Danny Federici

Bruce had played with Danny since 1968. It was a hard loss. In 2011, Clarence Clemons suffered a serious stroke at his home in Florida. As soon as Bruce

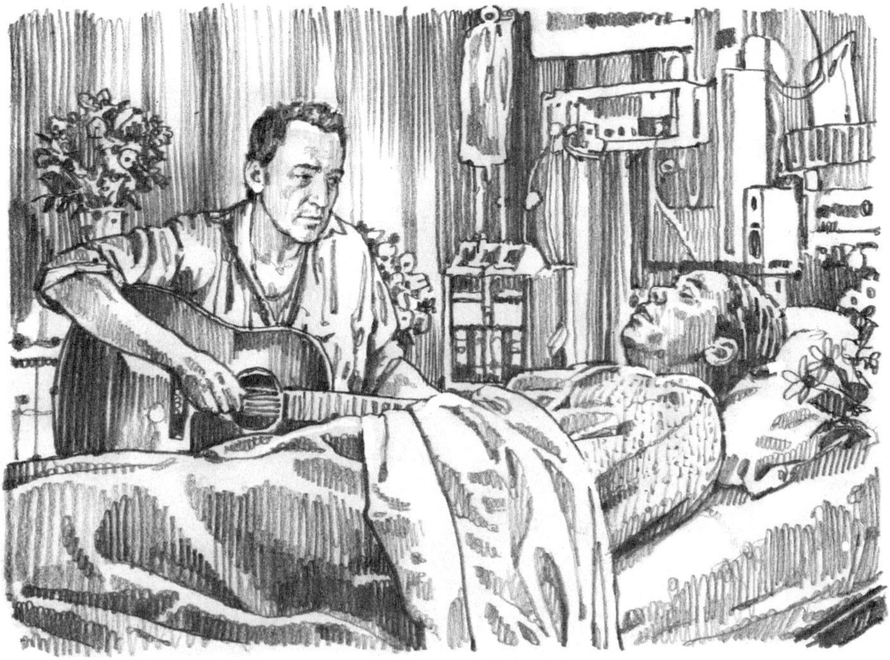

heard, he flew from Europe to be with him. He sat next to Clarence's bed and played the guitar for three hours. Clarence passed away soon after. At the funeral, Bruce spoke about the impact Clarence's friendship had on him. He said, "Clarence was big and he made me feel and think and love and dream big."

Even though Bruce's life was busy with music and tours, his children were always most important to him. When Bruce and Patti returned to the Jersey Shore in the mid-1990s, they raised their family only a short drive away from where Bruce had grown up. However, Bruce's kids had a very different childhood from their dad.

They had a big house and yard. Evan and Jessica both graduated from college, unlike their dad. Youngest child Sam became a firefighter in New Jersey, which made his father so proud.

As for Bruce, he kept on writing, but now he had new audiences. Bruce became an author. In November 2014, a picture book he wrote called *Outlaw Pete* was published. "Outlaw Pete" is also the name of one of Bruce's songs. In the story, a six-month-old baby goes on some adventures in the Wild West. Does that sound familiar? Bruce said that one reason he wrote the story was because of a book his mother had read him each night when he was a young boy—*Brave Cowboy Bill*. Even over sixty years later, Bruce used memories from his childhood in his art.

In March 2012, Bruce gave a speech at South by Southwest. South by Southwest (also known as SXSW) is a music, film, and tech festival held each year in Austin, Texas. People with new ideas come from all over the world to the festival. Bruce spoke to a large group of hopeful musicians. Many of them had listened to Bruce's music when they were growing up, just as a younger Bruce had listened to Elvis, Bob Dylan, and the Beatles. Bruce urged the crowd to play their music with all their hearts. He said, "And stay hard,

stay hungry, and stay alive. And when you walk onstage tonight to bring the noise, treat it like it's all we have. And then remember, it's only rock and roll."

Bruce Springsteen has released more than thirty albums that have sold over 120 million copies. He's won twenty Grammy Awards and

Bruce Springsteen with other Kennedy Center Honors winners in 2009

an Academy Award, and was voted into the National Rock and Roll Hall of Fame. Bruce is more than just a musician. Bruce is a leader, a poet, and a voice for the people. He is an American legend.

Timeline of Bruce Springsteen's Life

1949	Bruce Frederick Springsteen is born on September 23 in New Jersey
1965	Joins the Castiles, his first official band
1972	Signs with a major record label, Columbia
1973	*Greetings from Asbury Park, N.J.*, Bruce's first album, is released
1975	*Born to Run* is released and critics rave about the album
	Time and *Newsweek* magazines both feature Bruce on their covers
1985	*Born in the U.S.A.* is the best-selling album of the year
1989	The E Street Band breaks up
1990	Evan, the first of Bruce's three children, is born
1991	Marries his second wife and mother of his children, Patti Scialfa
1994	Wins an Academy Award for Best Song for "The Streets of Philadelphia" in the film *Philadelphia*
1999	Inducted into the Rock and Roll Hall of Fame
	The E Street Band reunites for a tour
2002	*The Rising* is released and sells over five hundred thousand copies its first week
2009	The E Street Band performs at the Super Bowl halftime show in Tampa, Florida
2012	Gives the keynote speech at SXSW Music Festival
2014	Releases his first picture book, *Outlaw Pete*

Timeline of the World

1940	Woody Guthrie writes "This Land Is Your Land"
1941	Bob Dylan is born in Minnesota
1945	Harry Truman becomes president of the United States
	World War II ends
1948	*The Ed Sullivan Show* first airs on TV
1964	The Beatles play their first show in the United States in Washington, DC
1968	US armed forces are attacked in the Tet Offensive in Vietnam, leading to more antiwar protests
1977	Elvis dies at Graceland, his Tennessee mansion, in August
1987	Austin, Texas, hosts the first SXSW Music Festival
1994	Tom Hanks wins the Academy Award for Best Actor for *Philadelphia*. Hanks plays a gay lawyer fighting AIDS
2001	Terrorists attack the United States on September 11
	Apple releases its first portable music player, the iPod
2003	The United States enters the Iraq War
2004	Facebook is launched by Mark Zuckerberg, a student at Harvard University
2008	Barack Obama becomes the first African American to be elected president of the United States
2012	Barack Obama is reelected as president

Bibliography

Burger, Jeff, ed. ***Springsteen on Springsteen: Interviews, Speeches, and Encounters***. Chicago: Chicago Review Press, 2013.

Carlin, Peter Ames. ***Bruce***. New York: Touchstone, 2012.

Dolan, Marc. ***Bruce Springsteen and the Promise of Rock 'N' Roll***. New York: Norton, 2012.

Heylin, Clinton. **E Street Shuffle: The Glory Days of Bruce Springsteen & The E Street Band.** New York: Viking Books, 2013.

Marsh, Dave. ***Bruce Springsteen: Two Hearts, the Definitive Biography 1972–2003***. New York: Routledge, 2003.

Springsteen, Bruce, and Frank Caruso. ***Outlaw Pete***. New York: Simon and Schuster, 2014.